BEAUTIFUL UNION

STUDY GUIDE

BEAUTIFUL UNION

STUDY GUIDE

A PRACTICAL COMPANION FOR DEEP
REFLECTION, GOOD CONVERSATION,
AND TOUGH QUESTIONS YOU REALLY
WANT TO ASK (BUT HAVEN'T YET)

JOSHUA RYAN BUTLER

MULTNOMAH

All Scripture quotations, unless otherwise indicated, are taken from the
ESV® Bible (The Holy Bible, English Standard Version®), copyright ©
2001 by Crossway, a publishing ministry of Good News Publishers. Used
by permission. All rights reserved. Scripture quotations marked (NIV) are
taken from the Holy Bible, New International Version®, NIV®. Copyright
© 1973, 1978, 1984, 2011 by Biblica Inc.™ Used by permission of
Zondervan. All rights reserved worldwide. (www.zondervan.com). The
"NIV" and "New International Version" are trademarks registered in the
United States Patent and Trademark Office by Biblica Inc.™

Published in the United States by Multnomah,
an imprint of Random House, a division of
Penguin Random House LLC.

MULTNOMAH® and its mountain colophon are registered trademarks of
Penguin Random House LLC.

This work is based on and directly quotes from *Beautiful Union*
by Joshua Ryan Butler, first published in trade paperback by Multnomah,
an imprint of Random House, a division of Penguin Random House LLC,
New York, in 2023, copyright © 2023 by Joshua Ryan Butler.

Trade Paperback ISBN 978-0-593-44505-1
Ebook ISBN 978-0-593-44506-8

The Cataloging-in-Publication Data is on file
with the Library of Congress.

Printed in the United States of America on acid-free paper

waterbrookmultnomah.com

1st Printing

First Edition

SPECIAL SALES
Most Multnomah books are available at special quantity discounts
when purchased in bulk by corporations, organizations,
and special-interest groups. Custom imprinting or excerpting can
also be done to fit special needs. For information, please email
specialmarketscms@penguinrandomhouse.com.

CONTENTS

Part IV
Union and Diversity

Part V
When God Says No

Part VI
A Greater Vision

Part VII
Triune Temple

HOW TO USE THIS GUIDE

Sex is designed to point to greater things. Big, beautiful things. That's the message at the heart of *Beautiful Union:* exploring how God's vision for sex points us to the good, unlocks the true, and (sort of) explains everything. This vision is for you, whether you're single or married, young or old—whatever your life circumstances. For in Christ, these grander realities are offered to us all.

This study guide is designed to help you dive more deeply into the key concepts of *Beautiful Union:* to reflect on them and make them your own, to creatively explore their significance from fresh new angles, to discuss those concepts with others or journal on their implications for your life, and to integrate God's beautiful vision into the intricacy of your own life and circumstances.

This guide is a companion to the book *Beautiful Union,* and it can be used individually or in groups (such as book clubs, discussion gatherings, and other kinds of small groups). When you use this guide alongside the book, it will help you—and your group, if you're a part of one—to get the most out of the content.

The guide is divided into seven sessions, with each session covering two or three chapters (called mini-sessions) from *Beautiful Union*. Each mini-session includes a brief re-introduction to the chapter followed by the same basic components: Unpack It, Use Your Imagination, and Reflect on It. (More on each component below.)

Although this guide is divided into seven sessions, go at your own pace. If you're using this book in a group study, then it might work best as a seven-week study with participants reading and reflecting on a few chapters each week. Or your group may decide to stretch it out to a fourteen-week study. Do what works best for your schedule and timeline.

Reading Schedule for *Beautiful Union*

If you haven't already read the book *Beautiful Union*, do so as you work your way through these sessions:

Session 1   Intro and Chapter 1
Session 2   Chapters 2–3
Session 3   Chapters 4–5
Session 4   Chapters 6–7
Session 5   Chapters 8–10
Session 6   Chapters 11–12
Session 7   Chapters 13–15

Unpack It

Here you'll encounter questions designed to help you recap, unpack, and cement key insights from each chapter. Use this space to record important takeaways, making them your own, so you can easily return to them later.

Use Your Imagination

These creative exercises are designed to help you reflect, using your imagination in unexpected ways, on a big idea from the chapter. These work best when you don't rush through them, so set aside ten to fifteen minutes, ideally, for each exercise. Take time to let your imagination explore the exercise and journal your reflections.

Reflect on It

These exercises are intended to guide you in reflecting on the significance of a central idea in your own life and what it might mean or look like to live in light of these big, beautiful realities you're exploring in the book.

Group Leaders

If you're completing this study in a group setting and you're the facilitator of your group, here are some simple guidelines that can help make this group journey through *Beautiful Union* more rewarding. Each session has enough content for sixty to ninety minutes of group time, depending on how long your group likes to spend in deeper discussion of each topic.

If you're part of an established small group going through *Beautiful Union*, your group is probably familiar with how to review content in workbooks and studies similar to this one. It may not be necessary to prescribe every detail of the group meetings, though this brief refresher may help you prepare for the group's discussion.

Review and Pray

Before meeting with the group, read the chapters of *Beautiful Union* associated with the upcoming session (see the reading schedule on the facing page) and complete the mini-sessions. Then pray for each person in your group and for your time together.

Group Members

Encourage every group member to read the assigned chapters of *Beautiful Union* and complete the sections in this guide before they arrive at the meetings each week.

Getting Started and Introduction

Once your group members have arrived, settle into a place free of distractions where you can sit comfortably for the next hour. Then, when you're ready to get started, ask a group member to read the mini-session's introduction aloud.

Unpack It

Ask someone else to read through the questions, one at a time, and allow group members to share the initial thoughts they wrote down.

Use Your Imagination

Give the group time to talk about the imagination exercise, offering space to share and unpack what they each wrote down.

Reflect on It

Encourage discussion of the responses in this section of the guide. As you lead your group through this guide, remember these pro tips:

- *Make time for each person to share.* The goal is to get everyone talking, to have everybody's voice heard and included as part of the discussion. This doesn't mean everybody needs to answer each particular question, but be mindful if certain people are dominating the discussion.

- *Don't make everyone share.* Sex is a sensitive topic. Some people might not be comfortable sharing their thoughts or experience, or they might still be processing and not be ready to share yet. Respect that. Don't pressure people to contribute who aren't ready or don't want to.

My hope is that by the end you'll have a bigger, more beautiful picture of God, the gospel, and the Christian vision for sex. I know I've been impacted tremendously by reflecting on the concepts at the heart of this book, and I hope you will be too.

In Christ,
Josh

PART I
SEX AS ICON

INTRODUCTION:
BEAUTY AND MYSTERY

Based on the introduction of *Beautiful Union*.

Takeaway: Sex is iconic.
It's designed to point to greater things.

---

*B*eautiful may not be the first word that comes to mind when you think of sex. Particularly the Christian vision for sex. *Backward. Bigoted. Outdated. Oppressive. Prudish. Puritanical.* These words are what many think of the traditional Christian sexual ethic today. But what if I told you *beautiful* can be the first word that comes to mind? That's the goal of this book: to restore the beauty of the Christian sexual ethic.

Sex is iconic. It's designed to point to greater things. That's the central thesis of this book. What do I mean by "icon"? Historically, icons were not meant to be looked *at* so much as to be looked *through*. They pointed to something beyond themselves. Sex can be an icon or an idol, either a window we look through to get a glimpse of the glory and goodness of God, or a mirror that reflects our selfishness, brokenness, and destruction.

The first step in restoring the beauty of Christian sexual ethics is to learn to look *through* sex to greater things. Throughout our exploration, we will discover that God is love. The love of God is the endgame of this book, for it's what the icon points to. God designed sex to reveal his love in technicolor.

Unpack It

1. When you think of Christian sexual ethics, what words first come to your mind? Is *beauty* one of them? Why or why not?

_____

_____

_____

_____

_____

_____

_____

2. Historically, icons were not meant to be looked *at* so much as to be looked *through*. They pointed to something beyond themselves. Sex is iconic. What do you think of this idea?

_____

_____

_____

_____

_____

_____

• Use the space below to make a list of some greater things you think God might have designed sex to point to, regarding the nature of our world and the life we were made for with God.

_____

_____

_____

_____

_____

3. Our culture has put sex in a "mega" place yet stripped it of its mystery. We've been trained by culture to look *at* sex but not to look *through* it. What are some ways you've seen a reduced vision of sex show up in our culture—that is, in movies, television shows, songs, or other areas of pop culture?

_____

_____

_____

_____

_____

- Do you find this vision for sex satisfying, or do you wish there were something more?

_____

_____

4. How might people around you describe the greater purpose of sex? Think of your friends and family, neighbors and co-workers. What words might they use to describe what sex is for?

_____

_____

_____

_____

_____

5. God designed sex to reveal his love in technicolor. How might sex be designed to point to the love of God? Describe some specific characteristics, in a healthy experience of sex, that might reflect aspects of God's love.

_____

_____

_____

_____

_____

6. What are some ways this image of love might get broken? Describe some specific practices or experiences that could break God's design for sex and fail to accurately reflect the love of God.

_____

_____

_____

_____

_____

_____

7. List at least one thing from the introduction that stood out to you or surprised you.

_____

_____

_____

_____

_____

_____

Use Your Imagination

Imagine you are a twelfth-century peasant in France. The printing press hasn't been invented, so you don't own a Bible. You've heard the stories of Scripture, but you are illiterate. When you visit your local church, however, you see an icon of _Christ Pantocrator._ The priest explains its symbolism to you.

1. What role might this icon play as a learning tool for your understanding of God?

_____

_____

_____

_____

_____

2. How might it function as a memory device for your imagination?

_____

_____

_____

_____

_____

_____

Like that twelfth-century peasant, our current culture is illiterate about God in many ways. Yet it's obsessed with sex. If God has embedded sex like an icon in the heart of our society . . .

3. How might reclaiming an iconic vision of sex deepen your understanding of God?

_____

_____

_____

_____

_____

_____

4. How might such a vision help those around you experience a fresh encounter with God?

_____

_____

_____

_____

_____

Reflect on It

Before embarking on this journey, take some time to pray about and reflect on any hopes, fears, or questions you might have. Feel free to include any parts of your story that relate to themes like sex, romance, marriage, family, and God. Here are some questions to consider:

What are your expectations for this study? What is one thing you're hoping to learn? A question you're hoping to answer? An experience you're hoping to heal? A theme you're hoping to discover?

Sex is a sensitive topic. What fears do you have? What are some unhelpful ways you've heard sex talked about that you hope to avoid as you progress through this guide?

_____

_____

_____

_____

_____

_____

_____

_____

_____

_____

_____

_____

_____

_____

_____

_____

_____

1

SEX AS SALVATION

Based on chapter 1 of *Beautiful Union.*

*Takeaway: Sex is an icon of salvation,
a sign of our union with Christ as his church.*

Sex wasn't designed to *be* your salvation but to point you to the One who is. It's not only the giving of vows at the altar but also what happens in the honeymoon suite after that speaks to the life you were made for with God. A husband and wife's life of faithful love is designed to point to greater things, but *so is their sexual union*! Sex is an icon of Christ and the church.

Christ arrives in salvation to be not only *with* his church but also *within* his church. Christ gives himself to his beloved with extravagant generosity, showering his love upon us, and imparting his very presence within us. Christ penetrates his church with the generative seed of his Word and the life-giving presence of his Spirit, which take root within her and grow to bring new life into the world.

Similarly, the church embraces Christ in salvation, celebrating his arrival with joy and delight. She has prepared and made herself ready, awaiting his advent in eager anticipation. She welcomes him into the most vulnerable place of her being, lavishing herself upon him with extravagant hospitality. She receives his generous gift within her—the seed of his Word and the presence of his Spirit—partnering with him to bring children of God into the world.

Their union brings forth new creation.

Unpack It

1. Read Ephesians 5:31–32. Paul says it's not only the *vows* of marriage ("leave and cleave") but also the *consummation* of marriage ("one flesh") that speaks to Christ and the church. Sex is an icon of salvation. This elevates the sacred significance of sex.

  • How does this iconic view of sex confront those in our churches who might see sex as dirty?

  _____

  _____

  _____

  _____

  _____

  • How does this confront those in our culture who might see sex as simply about personal pleasure?

  _____

  _____

  _____

  _____

  _____

  • Does this differ from your personal view of sex? If so, how?

  _____

  _____

  _____

  _____

  _____

2. Take a moment to consider how you've historically thought about sex, the male and female contributions to sexual union, and sexual desire. Use the space below to write out a few thoughts.

_____

_____

_____

_____

_____

• How is the idea that generosity and hospitality are embodied in the sexual act different from your original stance about male and female contributions to sexual union? How is it the same?

_____

_____

_____

_____

• How does desire as an icon of Christ's affection for his bride affect your view of male desire?

_____

_____

_____

_____

• How does desire as an icon of the church's longing to be romanced affect your view of female desire?

_____

_____

_____

_____

3. In what ways does sex as an icon of salvation create a fuller understanding of God for you?

_____

_____

_____

_____

_____

_____

4. The less extreme, tragic inversions of the iconic design are _____ and _____. What were your initial reactions to reading about these less extreme inversions?

_____

_____

_____

_____

_____

_____

• How have you experienced these lesser inversions in your own life or seen them played out in the lives of those you are close with?

_____

_____

_____

_____

_____

• How does it feel knowing that these are not part of God's design?

_____

_____

_____

_____

5. While marriage shows us the *shape* of the gospel, singleness shows us the *sufficiency* of the gospel.[1] How does an iconic vision support, rather than detract from, the sacred significance of singleness?

_____

_____

_____

_____

_____

_____

- What are ways the church has fallen short of this vision?

_____

_____

_____

_____

_____

- Why is it crucial that the church uphold a sacred vision for singleness?

_____

_____

_____

_____

_____

6. List at least one thing from this chapter that stood out to you or surprised you.

_____

_____

_____

_____

_____

Use Your Imagination

Take a moment to review the phrasing "one flesh" from the book (pages 6–7). Let's contrast the one-flesh union with some other (unbiblical) metaphors for salvation. To be clear, the following are *not* accurate visions of salvation. They are false, yet they represent approaches people often take to God. The point is to contrast the beauty of sexual union against the backdrop of these false images God has *not* chosen to use. Consider what each of these false metaphors would communicate about the nature of the gospel.

1. *Climbing the Sacred Mountain.* God sits atop a treacherous mountain. Athletes train their whole lives in preparation for the ascent. Only those who develop muscular strength, physical agility, and cardiovascular endurance can master the climb. On the appointed day, climbers race to the top. Those with injuries or disabilities are prevented from participating in the race. Many climbers die on the trek. Only those who make it to the top see the face of God and are awarded a new mansion to live in.

   • What does this metaphor imply about the nature of salvation?

   _____
   _____
   _____
   _____

   • In what ways does this metaphor contradict what God tells us about the one-flesh nature of salvation (see the discussion of Jesus as the pursuing God on page 14 of the book)?

   _____
   _____
   _____
   _____

- How does such grace change how you approach God?

_____

_____

_____

_____

2. *The Work Crew.* God sets prisoners free, breaking them out of captivity from their dark cells of solitary confinement. Once out in the light of day, however, they're immediately clothed in orange jumpsuits and put to work. They pick up trash, mow lawns, build playgrounds, construct homes, and help old ladies cross the street. Everyone is given a walkie-talkie so God can give them their new assignments every hour, on the hour. They never see God again but are given just enough food to have the energy to complete their assignments.

- What does this metaphor imply about the nature of salvation?

_____

_____

_____

_____

- In what ways does this metaphor contradict what God tells us about the one-flesh nature of salvation (see "In Defense of Romantic Worship Music" on page 19 in the book)?

_____

_____

_____

- How does such love change how you live with God?

_____

_____

_____

3. *The Popularity Contest.* Winners in a popularity contest are given elite access to the private network Life Hacks with the Savior. Every day, Jesus posts a new video with the hottest tips on diet, exercise, time management, romance, and more. Those who follow the daily regimen become smarter, faster, healthier, happier, and more attractive than their peers. While Jesus has never met them personally, he gives them all they need to live more satisfying lives.

- What does this metaphor imply about the nature of salvation?

  _____
  _____
  _____
  _____

- In what ways does this metaphor contradict what God tells us about the one-flesh nature of salvation (see "The Heart of Salvation" on page 17 in the book)?

  _____
  _____
  _____
  _____

- What does such security do to your heart and affection toward God?

  _____
  _____
  _____

Reflect on It

You were made for union with God. How does this differ from what you've previously understood about the point of the Christian life?

How is this a more beautiful picture of the nature of salvation than popular misunderstandings of Christianity? How can you hold on to sex as an icon of salvation to remind you of the life you were made for with God?

_____

_____

_____

_____

_____

_____

_____

_____

_____

_____

_____

_____

_____

_____

PART II
THE BEAUTY
OF SEX

2

WHY SUNSETS ARE BEAUTIFUL

Based on chapter 2 of *Beautiful Union.*

*Takeaway: Sex is an icon of creation,
a window into the structure of our world.*

M an and woman are introduced on the opening page of the
Bible. "Male and female he created them."[2] What's often
missed, however, is that they are not the only such pair. Genesis 1
introduces us to three other major mated pairs: heaven and earth,
land and sea, night and day. These pairs structure creation. While
each component is majestic on its own, guess where the most beautiful places in creation happen? *Where the two become one.*

Together, man and woman are a tiny template for our terrestrial
home, a window into the wonder of our enchanted world, a pint-
sized portrait of heaven and earth. When the two become one, their
convergence is a holy place, with the powerful potential to bring
forth both beauty and life. When they bring their diversity into
union, their interlocking bodies are embedded within an intertwined
universe. Swirling around us are heaven and earth, land and sea,
night and day. Sex is an icon of creation.

Love is the meaning of the world. This is the secret that sex reveals. Creation was made for diversity-in-union, and so were you.

You were made by love, in love, and for love—the love of your Creator. Sex is sacred because it's a sign that reveals this deep structure and purpose beneath the world. It's like a key that unlocks the truth of creation, opening us up to the mystery of the universe and the heartbeat of our Creator.

Unpack It

1. Genesis 1 is structured by complementary pairs, made with and for each other: heaven and earth, land and sea, night and day. When you sit at the intersection of one of the pairs, what goes through your mind? What are you feeling? Does one specific complementary pair hold a special place in your heart? Why? Use the space below to record your answers.

_____

_____

_____

_____

_____

_____

_____

2. *Beauty* and *life* characterize these intersections. People are drawn to these places where the two become one, regardless of whether or not they believe in God. How do these intersections point to something deeper given to us by God? What might that be?

_____

_____

_____

_____

_____

_____

- How can sex point to both the *beauty* of union and the *new life* that can emerge from it, as embedded in the structure of creation?

_____

_____

_____

_____

3. Heaven and earth are about more than just ozone and soil; they speak to God's sphere and ours. Jesus teaches us to pray for God's kingdom to come "on earth as . . . in heaven."[3] How does sex thus point to the in-breaking of God's kingdom?

_____

_____

_____

_____

_____

- What might this imply about the nature of God's kingdom? Describe some specific characteristics.

_____

_____

_____

_____

4. Love is the meaning of the world. This is the secret that sex reveals. Creation was made for diversity-in-union, and so were you. What do you think of this claim? Does it give you hope, and does it change how you see the natural world around you?

_____

_____

_____

_____

_____

5. *Sex* is not only a verb, but also a noun. You are sexed as an image bearer. What feelings and thoughts come to the surface knowing that your very being tells a larger story of love and belonging in the infinite presence of an eternal Creator?

_____

_____

_____

_____

_____

6. Christianity is not alone. A chorus of global voices sings of sex as a window into creation. It's striking how nearly universal this theme is among different traditions. How does this global chorus resonate with you? (Circle one answer below.)

It's inconsequential to me.

It reinforces the validity of the biblical picture.

Other: _____

7. How might this understanding—that sex is not simply an expression of the desires *within* you but has an objective grounding in the world *outside* you—change how you confront some common assumptions about sex in our culture?

_____

_____

_____

_____

_____

8. List at least one thing from this chapter that stood out to you or surprised you.

_____

_____

_____

Use Your Imagination

Congratulations! You've won a free vacation. A travel company is sending you and your closest loved ones on an all-expenses-paid trip. You get to choose three destinations. There's a catch, however: One destination must be a mountain, another a beach, and another a scenic locale from which to watch the sunset.

1. What three places would you visit? (Be specific: Not "the mountains" in general but "Mount Fuji" or "the Rocky Mountains." Not "the beach" but "the coast of Kauai.")

    Mountain: _____

    Beach: _____

    Scenic locale: _____

2. Why did you choose each place? What stands out about this destination in your imagination?

    _____
    _____
    _____
    _____
    _____
    _____

Sex is a window into the beauty of creation. People are drawn to the splendor of these places where the two become one.

3. Describe for your travel companions how God's vision for sex illuminates the grandeur of each of the three places you chose.

    _____
    _____
    _____
    _____

4. How does an iconic vision reveal the true nature of the world around us?

_____

_____

_____

_____

_____

_____

Reflect on It

Love is the meaning of the world. The icon of sex suggests that God's purpose for all creation—and God's purpose for _you_—is love. Reflect on the significance of this. How does this give you hope? What competing messages are you tempted to believe about the purpose of the world? Where do these competing messages come from? How can you remind yourself of God's purpose—the meaning of the icon—when these tough times hit?

_____

_____

_____

_____

_____

_____

_____

_____

_____

_____

_____

_____

3

LOVER, BELOVED, LOVE

Based on chapter 3 of *Beautiful Union.*

*Takeaway: The family is an icon of the Trinity,
as a tri-personal communion of love.*

Lover, Beloved, and Love has been a popular language for the Trinity throughout church history. The Father is the Lover, the Son the eternal Beloved, and the Spirit the unbreakable bond of Love between them. The family is designed to reflect this love of the Trinity in a way unlike any other kind of love in all creation. The family is made to be an icon of the most powerful truth in the universe: God is a communion of love.

Father, mother, and child are three persons sharing one substance and nature, imaging the triune life of God. The family makes love uniquely personal. Not only the lover but also the beloved and even the love itself are persons, all the way around. This reflects something of the Trinity, as a tri-personal communion of love. The love of God is expansive, generative, life-giving. That's what this aspect of the icon reveals.

Can you imagine living in perfect love? A circle of giving and receiving? Knowing and being known in secure relationship? Nothing to prove, no one to impress. Not needing to earn an identity or perform for your value and worth. You were made for this reality. You were made for this kind of love. You were made to belong.

Unpack It

1. There's a triune shape to love. The lover, beloved, and love are each present in the simple things, like enjoying a cup of coffee— where *you* are the lover, your coffee is the beloved, and love is the magnetic bond drawing its warm savory goodness toward your lips. What other simple things can you find the lover, beloved, and love in? Give two examples.

_____

_____

_____

_____

_____

_____

- How does this image of the triune compare to the Trinity, where the Lover, the Beloved, and even the Love are all persons? Where might it be lacking?

_____

_____

_____

_____

2. God has designed the family to reflect his divine love as Trinity, to image something of his own existence as a communion of persons. Why is it important to recognize that the family works as an analogy for the Trinity, rather than as an exact replica?

_____

_____

_____

_____

_____

3. You were made to belong. Describe the characteristics of a healthy family and how those characteristics speak to the kind of life you were made for as God's child.

_____

_____

_____

_____

_____

_____

- What are some ways healthy families get broken by our experiences in a fallen world?

_____

_____

_____

_____

4. Describe your family, growing up. How many siblings do you have, and where are you in the lineup? Did you grow up with both parents, one parent, or none?

_____

_____

_____

_____

_____

_____

- To the extent you feel comfortable, describe whether it was overall a good experience, a bad experience, or a mix.

_____

_____

_____

_____

_____

- When you compare your family with the icon, what parts of your story do you feel God might want to heal and restore?

  _____

  _____

  _____

  _____

5. Children are the "flesh and bone" of their parents. They receive their substance, nature, and image from their parents. How is this unity different from how you were taught about family?

  _____

  _____

  _____

  _____

  _____

  _____

- How does this elevate your understanding of the procreative nature of sex above other popular understandings today?

  _____

  _____

  _____

  _____

  _____

- Why do you think God providentially chose this way to create the human race?

  _____

  _____

  _____

  _____

  _____

6. God's love is expansive, generative, life-giving. How has the Holy Spirit been life-giving through your union with Christ?

_____

_____

_____

_____

_____

- What kind of fruit do you believe Christ wants to produce in you in the season ahead?

_____

_____

_____

7. The orgasm is a holy echo of triune joy. How does it shift your perception of God to see themes like joy and life-giving love at the heart of God's eternal life?

_____

_____

_____

_____

_____

- How does such an iconic window contrast with how culture trained you to think of the orgasm?

_____

_____

_____

8. List at least one thing from this chapter that stood out to you or surprised you.

_____

_____

_____

Use Your Imagination

1. Time to draw. While the African statue described on page 34 in the book depicts the family as diversity-in-union, often the family is seen more as separate individuals without a foundational union. In a drawing, represent this vision of the family as separate individuals. (Don't worry if you're a bad visual artist; just give it your best shot.)

• List some problems or dangers that can arise in this kind of family.

_____

_____

_____

_____

_____

_____

_____

_____

2. Some cultures can have a vision of the family that smothers the individual, overemphasizing the unity of the family in a way that eclipses their diversity as distinct persons. How would you represent this vision of the family in a drawing?

- List some problems or dangers that can arise in this kind of family.

_____

_____

_____

_____

_____

_____

_____

_____

3. Love confronts both *separation* and *smothering* (each fails to reflect triune love). Now take your best shot at drawing that African statue.

- List characteristics of a healthy family that avoids the dangers you listed above and more accurately reflects divine love.

  _____

  _____

  _____

  _____

  _____

  _____

  _____

  _____

4. Reflect on your family experience growing up. Which of your three drawings above most accurately reflects it? Describe specific aspects of your experience—good or bad—that relate to any of the three drawings.

_____

_____

_____

_____

_____

_____

Reflect on It

You were made to belong. You were made to know and be known in a secure communion of love, based not on your performance but on God's gift. You were made for an unbreakable communion of self-giving love. Use the space below to reflect on and answer the following questions.

What experiences in your family of origin have contradicted this message of the belonging that God made you for? Describe the message they implicitly communicated to you. How does God want to redeem those experiences and reshape your understanding of his heart toward you and the life you were made for with him?

_____

_____

_____

_____

_____

_____

_____

_____

PART III
LOVE AND LIFE

4

WEDDING ON A MOUNTAIN

Based on chapter 4 of *Beautiful Union*.

*Takeaway: Marriage is an icon of God's loyal love.
It's designed for covenant faithfulness.*

We use the word *love* a lot. "I love this iced tea." "I loved that movie." "Oh my gosh, I just *love* your shoes!" We're like a drunk Cupid, slinging amorous arrows at everything in sight. But when we dumb love down, our diminished definition becomes a far cry from the character of our Creator. Marriage is designed to display a love that is truly divine—and that can speak to us all, whatever our relationship status.

God is all-in. His love is faithful, relentless, and enduring. There's nothing we can do to earn it, no distance we can run to outpace it, no hurt we can inflict to break it. That's what weddings signify. God promises to never leave or forsake us, vowing to walk with us on the highlands above and in the valleys below, pledging through it all the security of his unfailing love.

Jesus is committed, promising to be with us through thick and thin, in good times and bad, in sickness and health, till death—nay, through death—when we're raised by his resurrected arms into his presence forever. A couple's ongoing devotion, living out their promises after the honeymoon ends, is designed to reflect Christ's unbreakable allegiance toward us. He will not run out on or betray us. We can take confidence in his unshakable loyalty and presence.

He's not going anywhere.

Unpack It

1. Think about a married couple you've looked up to. Describe what you've found inspiring about that couple's relationship.

_____

_____

_____

_____

_____

_____

2. *Hesed* is a difficult word to translate into English. List three characteristics of *hesed*, and describe how each one differs from mainstream conceptions of romantic love. (See "The Grammar of the Gospel" on page 50 in the book.)

- _____

- _____

- _____

3. *Falling in love* emphasizes love as _____, but God's *hesed*-style love is _____. What danger is there in approaching romantic love only the former way?

_____

_____

_____

_____

_____

_____

4. One of God's purposes for marriage is our spiritual formation.
How does this differ from popular notions of the purpose of
marriage in our culture?

_____

_____

_____

_____

_____

• Describe a few ways God could use marriage to form
someone into the image of Christ.

_____

_____

_____

_____

_____

5. Weddings are a window into a powerful truth: The Maker of the
universe wants to unite your life with his and live with you forever. What Old Testament event were Jewish wedding ceremo-
nies modeled on?

_____

_____

_____

_____

_____

6. What's the most extravagant wedding proposal someone you
know has done?

_____

_____

_____

_____

_____

- Describe what God promises in his covenant proposal to Israel.

_____

_____

_____

_____

- How does it compare to and contrast with the proposal you described?

_____

_____

_____

_____

7. Vows are a commitment to a life based on love. How do you think vows can provide stability for a couple?

_____

_____

_____

_____

_____

- What are some lesser ways people can approach vows today?

_____

_____

_____

- Does looking at the Ten Commandments as wedding vows for Israel change how you approach them? How so?

_____

_____

_____

_____

8. Weddings lay a foundation for a couple's future. Why do you think it's significant that the ceremony is public—before their family, friends, and community?

_____

_____

_____

_____

_____

_____

9. Describe a favorite wedding you've attended. What memories or symbols stand out from the day?

_____

_____

_____

_____

_____

• How might each element point to the union of Christ and the church?

_____

_____

_____

_____

_____

• What emotions surrounding that day might speak to God's heart toward us and the significance of our life with God?

_____

_____

_____

_____

_____

10. List at least one thing from this chapter that stood out to you or surprised you.

_____

_____

_____

_____

_____

_____

Use Your Imagination

Imagine you're back in elementary school, learning about nouns and action verbs. Think about how, as a child, you would have described _love_.

1. How would you have used _love_ in action in a sentence? Create three sentences based on actual experiences of being loved from your childhood. (For example, _My mom loved me by helping me with my homework._)

_____

_____

_____

_____

_____

_____

2. How would you have used _love_ as a feeling in a sentence? Create three sentences based on things you loved or people who loved you. (For example, _My dad loved watching me play baseball._)

_____

_____

_____

_____

_____

_____

3. Compare your culture's emphasis on romantic *love* as a noun with the biblical emphasis on *love* as a verb. What are the strengths of each, and what might you miss out on with only one or the other?

_____

_____

_____

_____

_____

Reflect on It

Whether you're single or married, Christ wants to unite your life with his and live with you forever. He will never leave you or forsake you. When you say yes to him, his commitment is to be with you through thick and thin, in good times and bad, in sickness and health—not even death will be able to separate you. Weddings are iconic of God's bold covenant love.

What relationships or experiences in your life have been characterized by instability rather than commitment, or conditional rather than unconditional love? (If helpful, think of your friends, church community, neighbors, co-workers, or social media network.) Describe the message they implicitly communicated to you. How does God want to redeem those relationships or experiences and reshape your understanding of his heart toward you and the life you were made for with him?

_____

_____

_____

_____

_____

_____

5

BRACE TO BE BORN

Based on chapter 5 of *Beautiful Union*.

*Takeaway: Procreation is an icon of God's kingdom,
where the Spirit brings forth new and abundant life.*

Jesus says his Father has loved him from all eternity.[4] This means that before God was Creator with a creation he had made . . . before God was Savior with our sin to save us from . . . before God was King with a kingdom to rule. . . . God has always been a Father loving his Son.[5] The love that flooded my heart at the birth of each of my children was a glimpse into the eternal love of God.

You were made for this kind of love.

Procreation is an icon of God's kingdom. It's not only the *unitive* aspect of sex that speaks to our life with God but the *procreative* as well. The New Testament uses every stage of procreation to describe the Spirit's work in our lives: conception, pregnancy, labor, birth, nursing, and child-rearing—even agricultural fruitfulness. If marriage speaks to our union with Christ, procreation speaks to our life from the Spirit.

The Spirit of God makes us children of God.

Unpack It

1. The New Testament uses imagery from every stage of procreation to describe the work of this person of the Trinity:

   _____

2. Jesus says that you must be born again to enter the kingdom, but this phrase has become cliché. Do you have any negative associations with the term *born again*? Describe them.

   _____
   _____
   _____
   _____
   _____

   • "Born again" can also be translated "born _____
     _____." (Refer to page 64 in the book.)

   • What epiphanies or paradigm shifts given in this chapter were meaningful for you and helped reclaim the significance of this term?

     _____
     _____
     _____
     _____

3. Conception speaks to our identity as God's children. How does 1 John 3:9 use the word *seed* (*sperma*) to describe our identity as God's children?

   _____
   _____
   _____
   _____
   _____

- What is semen associated with in modern cultural references? How does this understanding differ from the biblical meaning of *semen*?

_____

_____

_____

_____

- What would it look like to live your life knowing that God's seed remains in you?

_____

_____

_____

4. Creation is a pregnant mom. In Romans 8, what do "groaning" and "the pains of childbirth" describe?

_____

_____

_____

_____

- How is the pain of labor different from hitting your thumb with a hammer?

_____

_____

_____

_____

- How can this provide meaning and hope for painful areas of your life or for the broader suffering of our world?

_____

_____

_____

_____

5. Birth is an icon of resurrection. Jesus has gone before you, exiting the womb of the old creation into new-creation life. Imagine an infant's experience of being born, and describe which aspects you think can speak—metaphorically or literally—to what you will experience in the coming resurrection.

_____

_____

_____

_____

_____

• When a child is born, what emotions does a mother experience that might speak to the future hope of creation?

_____

_____

_____

6. The female body is iconic. It points to the maternal identity of the church, the life-giving power of the Spirit, and the hope of resurrection. What are some negative messages you've heard regarding the female body, whether in the church or in our broader culture?

_____

_____

_____

_____

• What kind of impact do you think these messages can have on women living under them?

_____

_____

_____

- What beautiful counter-messages most struck you from this chapter's discussion of the iconic nature of the female body?

_____

_____

_____

_____

7. Parenthood doesn't stop at birth. In many ways, the job has just begun. Similarly, the church's maternal identity includes raising up daughters and sons of God. What is breastfeeding used to represent in the New Testament? What about solid food?

_____

_____

_____

_____

- How can an iconic view of the church as mother help you distinguish good pastoral teaching and care from bad leadership?

_____

_____

_____

8. Make a (short) list of the places where you pay to be a member (that is, the gym, Netflix, and so on), and notate next to each one a membership benefit.

_____

_____

_____

_____

- What happens if you stop paying the membership dues?

_____

_____

- How is being a family member different from being a club member?

  _____

  _____

  _____

9. Using the space below, describe what you think the family of God should look like as the household of our heavenly Father. Take time to pray for your church in light of this vision.

   _____

   _____

   _____

   _____

10. List at least one thing from this chapter that stood out to you or surprised you.

    _____

    _____

Use Your Imagination

A UFO crash-lands in your backyard. Its pilot—an alien visitor— joins your Bible study and wants to learn about God. His species reproduces asexually, however, so all the procreative imagery in the New Testament confuses him. Using simple language, how would you describe each of the following stages of procreation to your new friend? Relate each to the work of the Spirit in our lives.

Conception: _____

Pregnancy: _____

Labor: _____

Birth: _____

Nursing: _____

Child-rearing: _____

Reflect on It

God's endgame is not to get something from you; it's to give life to you. To wrap you into his family and share his life with you. All your activity *for* God flows out of this reality *from* God. You were made to belong and ultimately to belong with God. You don't need to strive to ascend from below; you were made to be born from above. The Spirit of God wants to bring forth the life of God in you, to regenerate you and prepare you for resurrection life.

What areas of your life—such as physical, emotional, spiritual, relational—most need God's life-giving presence today? Take some time to name those things, bringing those areas of need before God and asking him to meet them.

_____

_____

_____

_____

_____

_____

_____

_____

_____

_____

_____

_____

_____

_____

PART IV
UNION AND DIVERSITY

6

CIVIL WAR AMPUTEES

Based on chapter 6 of *Beautiful Union.*

Takeaway: Divorce violates union,
depicting the shattering of our union with Christ.

Research says that divorce is one of the most difficult experiences
a person can endure. What makes divorce so painful? I want to
suggest here that the pain is embedded in something deeper than
simply divorce's impact on us. The trauma is not only what it does
to us but also what it says about God. Could it be that divorce is so
painful because it preaches a false gospel? Does it hurt so much because it speaks a lie about God?

Divorce shatters the icon. It is a witness to a world divided. If
marriage is an icon of creation, a stained glass window into the ca-
thedral of the world, then divorce displays an architecture built for
collapse, a universe where detachment, dissolution, and disintegra-
tion have the last word. A house divided against itself cannot stand,
and a crumbling couple images the collapse of our cosmic home. It is
a blueprint for a world where togetherness yields to separation,
communion gives way to isolation, and we wind up alone at the end.

Our salvation is insecure, it proclaims, for our union with Christ as
his bride is on rocky footing. The wedding feast of the Lamb shall

establish no final peace, we are told, for we live in a land where division has the final say. God abhors the death of a marriage because it takes this window into the hope of the world and cracks it at the center, turning the image of salvation into a fractured reflection of the fragmenting reality of sin. Divorce is a liar who symbolizes the greatest of horrors: the defeat of the gospel and the destruction of God.

Unpack It

1. Have you experienced divorce or walked closely with someone who has? To the extent you feel comfortable, describe what the experience felt like for you or your friend.

_____

_____

_____

_____

_____

- Why do you think divorce is so painful?

_____

_____

_____

_____

_____

2. Read Matthew 19:3–6. Jesus quotes from Genesis 1 and 2 when responding to a question about divorce. Why is it significant that Jesus roots his understanding of marriage in the structure of creation rather than the cultural norms of his time?

_____

_____

_____

_____

_____

3. Divorce illustrates the unraveling of creation (the separation of heaven and earth, land and sea, night and day) and the instability of salvation (the breakup of Christ and the church). How does this iconic significance shed light on why divorce is so painful?

_____

_____

_____

_____

_____

4. Jesus says God is the one who truly unites people in marriage ("what God has joined together"[6]). What difference does it make to approach marriage as a sacred union established by God in covenant, rather than simply a contract two people enter into of their own accord?

_____

_____

_____

_____

_____

• How does this view of marriage compare with your own view?

_____

_____

_____

_____

• What implications does approaching marriage this way have for the ultimate foundation of a marriage?

_____

_____

_____

_____

5. God hates divorce. What motivations might some people attribute to God because of his stance on divorce?

_____

_____

_____

_____

_____

- How does it change or enhance your understanding of God to see that his stance on divorce is motivated by his love?

_____

_____

_____

_____

- Describe some of the specific ways divorce can hurt those involved (the deserted, the deserter, the children, etc.).

_____

_____

_____

_____

_____

6. Many churches use the "three A's" to determine circumstances in which divorce might be permissible. List them here. (See page 89 in the book.)

- _____

- _____

- _____

There's a difference between something being _____ and it being _____.

7. Jesus's sexual ethic sets a high bar for his people in every culture, since it is rooted in the structure of creation. What are some ways Christians are tempted to lower the bar today?

_____

_____

_____

_____

_____

8. How is Jesus's cross and resurrection good news for those who've experienced divorce?

_____

_____

_____

_____

9. List at least one thing from this chapter that stood out to you or surprised you.

_____

_____

_____

Use Your Imagination

Day and Night's relationship has been rocky. Ever since that solar eclipse—when the moon held back the sun's ability to shine—their rhythm's been off. The magic just hasn't been the same: the chilling sideways glances Night gives in passing; the heated insults of Day that still burn. Now they're splitting over "irreconcilable differences." You're the judge, deciding who gets what in the divorce proceedings.

1. Which hemisphere does Night get custody of, and which does Day get custody of?

_____

_____

2. Describe the adjustments those living in each hemisphere must make to accommodate the perpetual darkness of Night and the unrelenting sunlight of Day.

_____

_____

_____

_____

3. If marriage is a window into the structure of creation, what kind of picture of the world does divorce present?

_____

_____

_____

_____

Reflect on It

Our union with Christ is secure, but other relationships can be unstable. Reflect on some of the relationships that have let you down. Even if not as extreme as divorce, name some of the experiences in which people have disappointed you when you were counting on them. Use the space below to bring those experiences before God. Bring him your pain—don't be afraid to grieve or cry if you need to—and ask him to minister to you, to heal those wounds, and to build an ever-increasing confidence in his secure reliability with and for you for eternity.

_____

_____

_____

_____

_____

_____

7

THE GREAT EXCHANGE

Based on chapter 7 of *Beautiful Union.*

Takeaway: Gay sex violates diversity.
It is unable to bear witness to the complementary
structure of creation and nature of salvation.

Sex embodies an iconic diversity that is central to God's heartbeat for the world. This includes both our sexual difference *as* male and female, and the sexual union *of* male and female. The biological reality of our anatomical particularity speaks, at a foundational level, to the diversity of our nature grounded in the structure of creation. Men and women are together an icon whose image-bearing bodies make a bold proclamation: God is pro-diversity.

The problem with gay sex, according to Romans 1, is that it violates this diversity. When man exchanges woman for a male sexual partner or vice versa, diversity is traded for uniformity, complementarity for similarity. We replace a window into our biological counterpart with a reflection of our mirrored self. And this is a symbol of something bigger.

Same-sex sexual activity becomes a window into a world of same-with-same, rather than difference-in-harmony. It is unable to bear witness to the beauty and life that mark heaven and earth, night and day, land and sea, the complementary pairs of creation. More significantly, it is unable to bear witness to the even greater diversity of Christ and church, the temple reality where divine and human come together in a union oriented toward the bringing of new life into the world.

Gay sex is an icon of *anti-diversity*.

Unpack It

1. The LGBTQ+ conversation is a sensitive one. Do you have any family or friends who identify as gay or lesbian? Describe what walking with them has been like. Or if you're comfortable sharing, has same-sex attraction been part of your story? Describe what the experience has been like for you.

_____

_____

_____

_____

_____

- What is the first thing LGBTQ+ people need to hear?

_____

_____

_____

_____

2. Romans 1 is saturated with creation imagery. List a few ways Paul uses creation as a backdrop in this passage. Why is that important?

_____

_____

_____

_____

_____

_____

- What did the phrase "against nature" refer to, when it came to sex, in the Greco-Roman world?

_____

_____

_____

_____

_____

3. The structure of Romans 1 is that of exchange. Use the space below to list the first two exchanges in Romans 1. These two exchanges are ways of describing what great exchange?

_____

_____

_____

_____

_____

_____

- How does the third exchange compare with the first two exchanges in how it disrupts the icon of creation?

_____

_____

_____

_____

_____

- What bigger point of Paul's argument does this break-down represent?

_____

_____

_____

_____

_____

_____

4. Diversity-in-union is central. Jesus says the problem with divorce is that it violates the _____ side of the equation; Paul says the problem with gay sex is that it violates the _____ side of the equation. Both Paul and Jesus appeal to _____ to make their case. (See page 95 in the book.)

5. God is pro-diversity. How does our *bodily* diversity, as male and female, run deeper than differences in desire?

_____

_____

_____

_____

_____

- How does God's delight in the diversity of his creation compare to and contrast with the message LGBTQ+ people sometimes hear from the church?

_____

_____

_____

_____

6. When it comes to sex as an icon of creation and salvation, what greater realities is gay sex unable to bear witness to?

_____

_____

_____

_____

_____

- On an iconic level, what does gay sex symbolically proclaim to the world?

_____

_____

- How does this proclamation contrast with what our broader culture proclaims about gay sex?

_____

_____

_____

7. American sexuality is like the *Titanic*. The problem with it is *much* bigger than gay sex. Focusing only on gay sex is like focusing on a leaky faucet on the *Titanic*. In your experience, what issues do Christians tend to focus on when it comes to sex, and which are they tempted to ignore?

_____

_____

_____

_____

_____

8. Romans 1 is also structured by three *give-overs*. What are these three give-overs, and how do they increase in intensity?

_____

_____

_____

_____

_____

- How have you seen these give-overs at play in your own life? (Remember Paul's aikido move in Romans 3:23: "All have sinned and fall short of the glory of God.")

_____

_____

_____

_____

- Paul's endgame in Romans 1 is to convict every person. How should this inspire a posture of humility

in us? How might you express that humility in the
way you talk about sex—and other ethical topics—with
others?

_____

_____

_____

_____

_____

9. When it comes to our union with Christ, what do you bring to
   the table? How does it differ from what Christ brings?

_____

_____

_____

_____

_____

_____

10. List at least one thing from this chapter that stood out to you or
    surprised you.

_____

_____

_____

_____

_____

_____

Use Your Imagination

You're on the *Titanic*. Water's breaking in through the hull; the
lower decks are flooded; the ship's going down. But there's a plot
twist: A rescue ship pulls up nearby. They ask you to help get passengers onto life rafts.

While scouring the cabins for remaining passengers, you come across Ralph. He's fixated on trying to repair some broken pipes flooding a room on an upper deck. Back home, Ralph's a plumber, and he thinks he can stop the leak if he just has more time.

1. What do you tell Ralph? How do you try to convince him to leave the cabin and board the rescue ship?

_____

_____

_____

_____

_____

American sexuality is the *Titanic*; Jesus's kingdom is the rescue ship.

2. Why is it important that you can point not simply to the problems in your culture (the *Titanic*) but to the beauty of Jesus's vision (the rescue ship)? What dangers have you seen when someone doesn't?

_____

_____

_____

_____

_____

Reflect on It

1. God loves diversity. He created you in all the particularity of who you are, and he created you for beautiful union with him. Are there any sexual desires you're struggling with? Perhaps it's the desire for pornography, for sex with someone who's not your spouse, or for same-sex sexual activity. Perhaps you're single and don't want to be, and are hungry for deep intimacy and connection. Perhaps you're married and lonely, craving affection

and validation from someone outside your marriage. Get honest and describe those desires here.

_____

_____

_____

_____

_____

_____

_____

_____

2. Rather than simply giving in to those desires (doing whatever you want, in spite of God) or repressing those desires (stuffing them through sheer willpower or pretending they're not there), redirect them to God. Ask Christ to fill you and fulfill you with himself, meeting your deepest desires with the presence of his Spirit, satiating your longings with intimate connection to him. Use the space below to write out your prayer. Afterward, consider picking a favorite worship song or calming music, putting on your headphones, and going for a walk—to rest in and worship the One your heart was made for.

_____

_____

_____

_____

_____

_____

PART V
WHEN GOD SAYS NO

8

SEX ISN'T CHEAP

Based on chapter 8 of *Beautiful Union*.

Takeaway: Premarital sex violates God's covenantal love. It fails to reflect God's all-in commitment to us before uniting with us.

God commits to us before he unites with us—and calls us to do the same. Christ is not just out to *sleep* with his church but to *marry* his church! Wedding your spouse before bedding your spouse images God's covenantal love. God's vision is for an "all of life" union marked by faithfulness, commitment, and permanence. The problem with premarital sex is that it violates this covenantal love of God.

Premarital sex preaches a false gospel. It reflects a God who is not all-in, who is not fully committed to us. It images a Christ who is unwilling or ashamed to proclaim his devotion to us before the watching world. It fails to reflect God's faithful, relentless, and enduring love and the security of our life in his divine embrace. It's wrong not just because it breaks a rule but because it fails to accurately image God.

God invites us to move from rule keeping to image bearing—not to simply jump through the hoops to try to keep him happy or to get a blessing but rather to seek to be formed by his character and accurately bear his image to the world. The goal of sexual purity is not to *make* God love you; it's to *reflect* the purity of God's great love for you. The endgame is much deeper than rule keeping. It's *image bearing*.

Jesus is committed to us, and our love lives are meant to reflect that.

Unpack It

1. How do your friends and peers tend to think about premarital sex?

_____

_____

_____

_____

_____

- In their opinion, what is the goal of sex?

_____

_____

- What requirements, if any, do they think should be in place before a couple has sex?

_____

_____

_____

_____

2. If you were familiar with purity culture before reading this chapter, what was your experience or impression of it?

_____

_____

_____

_____

_____

- Purity culture has been referred to as a "sexual prosperity gospel." What's wrong with using an if-then formula to motivate sexual faithfulness?

_____

_____

_____

_____

_____

3. The goal of sexual purity is not to *make* God love you; it's to *reflect* the purity of God's great love for you. Describe the difference between rule keeping and image bearing as an approach to sexual faithfulness.

_____

_____

_____

_____

_____

_____

- Have you had a rule-keeping mindset in the past? If so, describe it.

_____

_____

_____

_____

- What is your initial reaction when someone sets a hard boundary for you?

_____

_____

_____

_____

- How does a truer understanding of image bearing provide deeper intimacy with God and a stronger motivation for faithfulness? Jesus says his yoke is easy and his burden light;[7] how does image bearing lighten the load when it comes to sexual faithfulness, compared with a rule-keeping mindset?

  _____

  _____

  _____

  _____

  _____

- What role do the rules still play in image bearing?

  _____

  _____

  _____

  _____

4. "Leave and cleave," the wedding formula of Genesis 2:24, refers to both the human covenant of marriage and God's covenant with us. What aspects of God's character can sexual faithfulness reflect to your spouse and to the world?

  _____

  _____

  _____

  _____

  _____

- How does premarital sex misrepresent the character of God and the heart of the gospel?

  _____

  _____

  _____

  _____

- Jesus "left his father and mother" and "cleaved to us" in the gospel. How does this change the significance of sex for you? Premarital sex?

_____

_____

_____

_____

5. Birth control and high-resolution pornography have had a radical impact on the relationship market of society. Which natural aspect of sex does each "market disruptor" sever sex from?

_____

_____

_____

_____

- Which of these two market disruptors stands out the most to you in its impact on people's relationship to sex?

_____

_____

_____

- What kind of impact have you seen it make in your own circle of friends?

_____

_____

_____

6. Valuable things are a target. Why should you guard and uphold a high vision of sex?

_____

_____

_____

_____

- What are some ways you can hold on to the holy vision for sex?

  _____

  _____

  _____

7. List at least one thing from this chapter that stood out to you or surprised you.

  _____

  _____

  _____

Use Your Imagination

Imagine an alternate world where marriage doesn't exist. Even more, while the government encourages sexual activity, it prohibits couples from staying together longer than two years—in the interest of promoting sexual experimentation and diversity of experience. Here's one more curveball: There's no birth control.

1. How do you imagine men and women interact with and view one another in this brave new world?

  _____

  _____

  _____

  _____

  _____

2. What emotional and psychological impact does this have? What difference, if any, is there in how this scenario tends to affect women versus men?

  _____

  _____

  _____

  _____

3. What is life like for children in this world?

_____

_____

_____

_____

_____

While our modern world is (thankfully!) not as extreme as this alternate world, describe any similarities you observe in how people tend to approach sex today and the impact of this approach on society.

4. How do men and women tend to interact with and view one another today in the relationship market of society?

_____

_____

_____

_____

_____

5. What emotional and psychological impact does this have? Is there a difference in how the relationship market today tends to affect women versus men?

_____

_____

_____

_____

_____

6. Are children vulnerable in any unique ways today? If so, how?

_____

_____

_____

_____

_____

Reflect on It

God's great love for you is pure, committed, loyal, true—and valuable beyond compare. *That's* what you're being invited to image, in both your sexuality and your relationships more broadly. Reflect on God's great love for you. Use the space below to thank God for who he is and what he's done in your story. Include specific details of who he's revealed himself to be in Scripture and specific experiences or people in which his love has shown up in your life.

End by asking him to empower you to reflect his divine love in your relationships, to move from rule keeping to image bearing, to be sexually pure and faithful to Jesus in your romantic relationships, and to embody the strength of his love with those in closest proximity to you.

9

CHEATING ON GOD

Based on chapter 9 of *Beautiful Union*.

Takeaway: Adultery violates faithfulness.
It reflects a breaking of divine covenant love.

A dultery is *brutal.* The problem is not only what it does to your spouse—as horrible as that is—but also what it says about God. If premarital sex violates the covenantal nature of God's faithful love, adultery violates the faithful nature of God's covenant love. If premarital sex refuses to enter covenant, adultery breaks the covenant one has entered.

Infidelity infiltrates the icon, disfiguring and distorting the divine reflection of faithful love (*hesed*) at the heart of the One it was meant to represent. Adultery images a God who is unfaithful—and that is simply not true. It cuts against the grain of the universe, reflecting a false god. It preaches a false gospel, betraying the divine character embedded in the icon of marriage. To lie with another is to lie about God.

Infidelity is the Bible's most frequent depiction of sin. It's an intriguing image, for it speaks to a betrayal of trust—intimate and relational. It involves giving yourself to another, in departure from the One you were made for. While wickedness can take on many forms, and evil is ineffable and difficult to describe, at its core our crime is adultery.

Sin is cheating on God.

Unpack It

1. Have you experienced infidelity or known someone who has? To the extent you're comfortable sharing, describe the circumstances and emotions connected to the experience. If you haven't, why do you think adultery is so painful?

_____

_____

_____

_____

_____

_____

2. Adultery is the Bible's primary picture to represent sin. What does this say about the type of relationship you were made for with God?

_____

_____

_____

_____

_____

_____

• What does this say about the nature of our violation?

_____

_____

_____

_____

_____

• What two things in our relationship with God does the Bible characterize as adultery?

_____

_____

3. God is jealous for his bride. He doesn't want to share your *ultimate* affection with any other thing—even good things. How does it make you feel to know that God is jealous for you?

_____

_____

_____

• What does this say about the nature of God's love for us?

_____

_____

_____

_____

• What does it look like to keep him first in your life?

_____

_____

_____

_____

4. In Exodus 32–34, God displays something similar to the stages of grief some go through after experiencing adultery. What insight might God's reaction to Israel's infidelity offer people who've been cheated on?

_____

_____

_____

_____

_____

5. What was the double standard in the ancient world, and why did it exist? How does God confront it in the Old Testament?

_____

_____

_____

_____

_____

- Do you still see the double standard around today? If so, how?

_____

_____

_____

_____

- How does the gospel confront the double standard?

_____

_____

_____

_____

6. What hope is there in God for those who've been cheated on and for those who've committed adultery?

_____

_____

_____

_____

_____

7. List at least one thing from this chapter that stood out to you or surprised you.

_____

_____

_____

_____

_____

Use Your Imagination

1. We could use a variety of images for evil. Jot down what each of the three images below communicates about the nature of sin by considering the following questions: Who is God in this picture? What is God's character and the nature of his claim on us? Who do we, as humanity, represent in the scenario? What is our character and the nature of our violation?

   • Rebellion Against a King

   _____

   _____

   _____

   • Disease That Infects the Social Body

   _____

   _____

   _____

   • Vandalism Against the Flourishing of a Community

   _____

   _____

   _____

2. As mentioned before, adultery is the Bible's most prevalent image for sin. Reflect on what adultery represents in the biblical story, and briefly describe what this says about God's heart for you and his desire in his relationship with you. In what situations are you most tempted to stray from that love?

   _____

   _____

   _____

   _____

   _____

Reflect on It

God's love is faithful, but human love is often not. Reflect on ways you've experienced betrayal or been let down by those close to you. It doesn't have to be as extreme as adultery, though it can be. It doesn't have to be related to a romantic relationship, though it can be. The bigger theme here is betrayal.

Use the space below to name the hurt and disappointment, and bring them before God through prayer. Don't rush through this: Grief and lament are spiritual practices, and God truly cares about the depths of your heart. You can bring the weight of your disappointment to Jesus.

After exploring those depths, ask the Spirit of God to minister to you. Is the Spirit exposing a lie from that experience that the Enemy is using to deceive you about your worth and value? Is there a truth about how God sees you—your worth and value in Christ, the security and stability you have in him—that the Spirit wants to speak into your life? Ask him to speak, whether through an image, a verse, an impression, or a word that resonates with the truth of the gospel and of Scripture, and take some time to listen.

_____

_____

_____

_____

_____

_____

_____

_____

_____

_____

10

WELCOME THE CHILDREN

Based on chapter 10 of *Beautiful Union.*

*Takeaway: Adoption is an icon of the gospel,
displaying God's redemptive posture toward hurting children,
broken families, and a fallen world.*

Too many children today face abandonment, abuse, and neglect. Children are an icon of God's kingdom, but the alternative kingdom of darkness tears too many children down through no fault of their own. It's no surprise, then, that God is all about adoption. God is "a father to the fatherless," the psalmist sings, who "sets the lonely in families."[8] This means adoption is not just something God recommends; it's something God does. It's a window into his redemptive response to a fallen world.

Adoption is different from biological birth, however. It's always a response to some kind of tragedy. While natural birth is embedded in the structure of creation, the need for adoption arises only because the world has been torn apart by sin. It is thus a window into the reality of the Fall. In our broken world, we are all orphaned, destitute, and alone—in one way or another—alienated from our existential belonging and transcendent purpose. God's not out to simply make you a better citizen; he's out to make you family. The goal of the gospel is our adoption.

Adoption works. Your salvation depends on it. In Christ, you are truly a daughter or son of your heavenly Father, grafted into his family tree. You can take confidence in your identity, inclusion, and belonging. He has brought you in and established you, permanently, as his child. There is nothing that can take away his love for you. No mistreatment from a parent, no lie from the Enemy, no power of hell, can separate you from your belonging in the family of God.

Unpack It

1. Do you know anyone who was adopted, whether a family member, a friend, or yourself? Was the experience good, bad, or a mix of both? Why? If you don't know anyone, try to imagine which aspects would be hard and which would be redemptive.

_____

_____

_____

_____

_____

2. Read Ephesians 1:3–6. What stands out to you from this majestic description of how God does adoption?

_____

_____

_____

_____

- How does this compare to and contrast with the way you think of adoption?

_____

_____

_____

_____

- What does this say about how God sees you and your identity in him? Does it differ from what you assumed about God? How so?

_____

_____

_____

3. What did adoption signify legally in Roman culture, and how does it relate to your identity as a child of God?

_____

_____

_____

_____

_____

4. Adoption is different from biological birth. Birth is in the order of _____; adoption is an icon of _____. (See page 142 in the book.) Why is it important, in practical terms, to recognize that adoption is a response to a tragedy?

_____

_____

_____

_____

_____

5. Abortion is a sensitive topic. Do you feel comfortable or intimidated talking about it with others? Describe why. (Feel free to share any of your background story, reasons, or concerns, to the extent you feel comfortable.)

_____

_____

_____

_____

_____

- What is the central philosophical question in the abortion debate?

_____

_____

_____

_____

6. Have you ever been called names or felt dehumanized in a conversation? How so?

_____

_____

_____

_____

_____

- Why does what you call people matter?

_____

_____

_____

_____

7. In the symbolic order, what does abortion depict about the new creation?

_____

_____

_____

_____

_____

- Does this iconic view affect your perception of abortion? How so?

_____

_____

_____

_____

- Reflect on the symbolic depth of a hope-filled view of birth. Does it affect your perception of birth? How so?

_____

_____

_____

_____

8. Adoption is one way to fight abortion. List three ways you and your church can support at-risk children and their mothers. If you're already offering support, how is it working? What changes or additions might you consider, if any, based on what you learned in this chapter?

_____

_____

_____

_____

_____

9. How can you be pro-grace toward those for whom abortion is a part of their story or those facing a difficult decision today?

_____

_____

_____

_____

_____

10. Is there a person or family you know—such as a foster or adoptive family—that you can love and support in a tangible way this week? If not, what organization can you reach out to and offer help?

_____

_____

_____

_____

_____

11. List at least one thing from this chapter that stood out to you or surprised you.

_____

_____

_____

_____

_____

Use Your Imagination

Pretend with me for a moment: Society is now run on a social credit system. After every interaction you have, you can use a phone app to rank the person you interacted with. (Yes, this is like that _Black Mirror_ episode.[9]) A friend helped you move into your new house? They get five stars. That barista didn't smile when she gave you your coffee? Three stars. Have some hang-ups with how your parents raised you? One star. A high ranking gives you access to better neighborhoods to live in, leisure travel, and more affluent friends.

1. In this society, how do people act toward one another? What motivations drive them?

_____

_____

_____

_____

_____

2. What insecurities lurk inside them? Is this a society you would want to live in? Why or why not?

_____

_____

_____

_____

_____

While an extreme metaphor, this depicts a works-religion world, where you must perform to belong.

3. What parallels do you see between this scenario and the pressures of modern society?

_____

_____

_____

_____

_____

4. Have you felt any of these pressures yourself? Describe how.

_____

_____

_____

_____

_____

5. How is God's heart for family—biological, adoptive, and church—a window into a different kind of world, where belonging is based not on the performance of works but on the foundation of grace?

_____

_____

_____

_____

_____

Reflect on It

You were made to belong, based not on your performance but on God's grace. Reread Ephesians 1:3–6. Reflect on what it means that God *chose* you in Christ, that he *wants* you. What tragedies in your life have left you feeling like you're on your own, like you don't belong? Are there areas in your life where you feel the pressure to perform in order to be accepted, valued, or have worth? What confidence is God inviting you into as his child, and what would it look like for you to live into that reality?

_____

_____

_____

_____

_____

_____

_____

_____

_____

_____

_____

_____

_____

_____

_____

PART VI

A GREATER VISION

11

SPLITTING THE ADAM

Based on chapter 11 of *Beautiful Union.*

Takeaway: Sex is an icon of our interdependence.
Humanity's existence is intertwined, in the very substance of our
being, through the diversity-in-union of male and female.

God makes Adam and Eve differently—not just *anatomically* different but using a different *process.* Adam is made from the ground; Eve is made from Adam. This difference is significant. There is an organic unity to the human race. We are *inter*dependent—not independent—creatures. You need both sexes to exist, literally. Without your mom and dad, you wouldn't be here. We need each other. Our lives originate from prior union, emerging from the merger of the sexes. Your existence is bound up within the broader communion of our ancestral family tree.

This means that you are inextricably connected to an eighty-nine-year-old Chinese grandmother living in Beijing, to a twenty-four-year-old migrant worker in the fields of Nigeria, and to my daughter and sons here in Phoenix, Arizona. You are integrally connected to the human family tree through the sexual union of your ancestors, who have brought you into existence. Our lives are all connected, across space and time, arising against a backdrop of union.

Sex is more than simply a union; it is a *re*-union. It's a "getting the band back together," as the two sides of the icon—the corresponding halves of humanity—reunite as one. Men and women are, together, a window into the interdependent nature of the human family. Within the multicolored tapestry of the international social body, the threads of women and men interweave to mutually reinforce, beautifully build on, and together compose the fabric of the whole. All humanity is connected; we are flesh and blood.

Sex is an icon of one family of humanity.

Unpack It

1. Read 1 Corinthians 11:11–12. Reflect on the broader lesson of interdependency. What do you think of the idea that men and women need each other, beyond just procreation, to flourish?

   _____

   _____

   _____

   _____

   _____

   _____

   • Imagine a world where all people were men or all were women. What strengths do you think humanity as a whole might miss out on?

   _____

   _____

   _____

   _____

   _____

2. The alternate creation story (Jimmy on Fiji; Jenny on Hawaii) would be a story of primordial _____; Genesis 2, in contrast, is a story of primordial _____. (See page 157 in the book.)

- What does this say about our connection to others throughout history and around the globe?

  _____

  _____

  _____

  _____

- How does this change your perception of your neighbors? Your co-workers? The people at the grocery store?

  _____

  _____

  _____

  _____

- How might this change your interactions with others?

  _____

  _____

  _____

  _____

3. Adam rejoices that Eve is _____ of his _____ and _____ of his _____. In the Hebrew language, what does this mean?

   _____

   _____

   _____

   _____

4. What does the word "rib" (*tsela*) mean every other time it's used in Scripture, and what location is it generally associated with?

   _____

   _____

   _____

- What does this "hyperlink" suggest about the significance of Eve's creation?

_____

_____

_____

_____

5. Man and woman are, together, a temple. This means there is something sacred about sex, as a window into greater realities of God and his purposes for the world. How might such temple imagery invest sex with sacred meaning?

_____

_____

_____

- Describe some examples of a less-than-sacred mentality and approach to sex in our culture.

_____

_____

_____

_____

- What would it look like to treat sex as sacred?

_____

_____

_____

_____

6. The Hebrew term for "suitable" (*kenegdo*) combines notions of both sameness and difference. Which do people around you tend to emphasize more: the *sameness* of men and women or our *difference*?

_____

_____

• What might be the strengths and weaknesses of each approach?

_____

_____

_____

_____

7. List at least one thing from this chapter that stood out to you or surprised you.

_____

_____

_____

_____

_____

Use Your Imagination

Read the following three stories about how God could have chosen to create the first humans. Think about what message each of these stories would convey about God's purpose for sex.

1. *The Factory.* God built a large industrial factory, with smoke billowing from chimneys atop a dreary gray building. Inside, children are mass-produced. Men and women are brought quickly together on an assembly line—with only their genitals allowed to touch—then removed as soon as the deed has been done.

• What is the primary—perhaps the only—purpose of sex in this story?

_____

_____

_____

_____

_____

- What else might it imply about our purpose as humanity and how we relate to one another?

  _____

  _____

  _____

  _____

2. *The Jungle.* God placed the first men and women on teams in a jungle. The men had to battle the men, and the women had to battle the women, to see who would emerge victorious. The winning man and woman were then brought together, out of this hostile environment, to meet for the first time and marry.

- What is the primary purpose of sex in this story?

  _____

  _____

  _____

  _____

- What else might it imply about our purpose as humanity and how we relate to one another?

  _____

  _____

  _____

  _____

3. *The Castle.* God placed the first men and women in a castle, where they were provided with the choicest foods and the finest wine. They were surrounded by the ambience of romantic music with free rein to flirt, date, and sleep together. Once children were conceived, however, the couple was separated and forced to leave the castle. For their younger years, children were raised by their mothers (like Wonder Woman's Amazonian tribe). Upon reaching puberty, youth were transferred to spend adolescence with their fathers, never to see their mothers again.

- What is the primary purpose of sex in this story?

_____

_____

_____

_____

_____

- What else might it imply about our purpose as humanity and how we relate to one another?

_____

_____

_____

_____

4. Read Genesis 2. Contrast the biblical story of Adam and Eve's creation with the stories above.

- What is distinct from the first story of the factory?

_____

_____

_____

_____

- How about the second story of the jungle?

_____

_____

_____

_____

- What about the third story of the castle?

_____

_____

_____

_____

• Which story do you find most compelling, and why?

_____

_____

_____

_____

Reflect on It

You were made to be interdependent with others. This is different from *co*-dependence (where the uniqueness of who you are is absorbed or squashed by the other person) and different from *in*dependence (where you live autonomously and don't need other people). Take some time to reflect on which danger you tend toward more. Is your life marked by one of these tendencies in this season?

If so, bring this before God and ask him what it might look like for you to move closer to an *inter*dependent life in the season ahead. If not, take time to thank God for people (friends, family, or others) you've been blessed to live interdependently with. Be specific, naming the people, and consider both thanking God for them and praying for them (for example, that they might more deeply experience God's grace, peace, and love, or encounter God profoundly in their particular circumstances in this season).

_____

_____

_____

_____

_____

_____

_____

_____

_____

12

TRIUNE SYMPHONY

Based on chapter 12 of *Beautiful Union.*

*Takeaway: The family is made in the image of
the triune God, with a diversity-in-union that reinforces the
purpose of humanity—to reflect divine love.*

Genesis 1 is all about diversity-in-union. Earlier in this book, we saw how male and female are a window into the complementary pairs of heaven and earth, land and sea, night and day, which bring beauty and life into the world. Here in Genesis 1's climactic poem, we see that diversity-in-union is an icon of something much more: not only the structure of creation but also the identity of our Creator. The human family is mysteriously wrapped up somehow, this poem suggests, with the image of God.

Father, mother, and child share a three-in-oneness, like a musical chord, a triad of notes distinct yet united as participants in a symphonic whole. The family is made for harmony, and the triune God reveals that the melody we are designed to revolve around is love. Humanity was made to reflect the image of God *together*, through the symphony of our shared life, revolving around the melody of divine love, performed in collective concert into the world.

Sex is how *the Adam* gets built. The family expands and unfolds the one human race, generating other image bearers who share in the corporate image of God. It is through the sexual union of male and female that babies are made and the human social body grows on the earth. *The Adam* is like a lumbering giant who rises up from the ground, his body enlarging beneath him through the sexual union of his citizens, increasing in size through the intermingling of his members, generating the nations like growing legs with which to stand on the globe.

Family is how the "one image" expands and unfolds into the earth.

Unpack It

1. What's your favorite style of music? Name a favorite band or song or your favorite instrument to listen to, and describe what you like about this kind of music.

_____

_____

_____

_____

- Why do you think harmony and music are so powerful?

_____

_____

_____

_____

2. The family has a triune shape: Father, mother, and child share a three-in-oneness and are created for harmony. In Genesis, how does God make the one into two? How did the two then return back to one?

_____

_____

_____

_____

_____

- What biblical phrase speaks to a husband and wife sharing a two-in-oneness?

  _____

  _____

  _____

- How does the biblical phrase "flesh and bone" speak to the three-in-oneness of a child's relationship to their parents?

  _____

  _____

  _____

- Take a moment to think about your family history. Do the biblical phrases and meanings above reflect your experiences? Why or why not?

  _____

  _____

  _____

- What truths about God's design can either reinforce or restore your understanding of familial bonds?

  _____

  _____

  _____

3. People tend to think of the image of God as an *individual* thing, but it is also a *corporate* thing that all humanity shares. How does this help explain what sin broke and what Jesus is out to fix and restore?

  _____

  _____

  _____

  _____

  _____

- What might it look like for Jesus to unite the human family?

  _____

  _____

  _____

- What could it look like for the symphony to be restored in your community? In your church?

  _____

  _____

  _____

4. How do the pronouns in the "image of God" poem[10] emphasize both *diversity* and *union*?

   _____

   _____

   _____

   _____

5. What two meanings does *adam* have in Hebrew? What relevance does this joint meaning have for the diversity-in-union theme of the poem?

   _____

   _____

   _____

   _____

6. If the family is the foundation of civilization, what does this say about God's heart for healthy families and their importance for the future of society?

   _____

   _____

   _____

   _____

- What does the triune structure of the human family say about how humanity was designed to collectively represent God in the world?

_____

_____

_____

- Where do you think we are collectively succeeding in this representation? Where do you think we are collectively failing?

_____

_____

_____

_____

7. Genesis 2 sings of the first human family in a way that powerfully resonates with classical Trinitarian theology. Eve and Seth proceed *from* Adam, and all share one *nature* (human) and *substance* (flesh and bone) as family. How does this *unity* of the family—through life-giving oneness—compare to or contrast with how you've thought of the family?

_____

_____

_____

_____

_____

- How does this *sacredness* of the family—made to represent the highest reality of God—compare to or contrast with how you've thought of the family?

_____

_____

_____

_____

- How does the "not good" of our first father Adam's aloneness—with an inability to reflect the Father's life of communion in eternity—speak to your deep human need, whether single or married, for rich relationships and community?

_____

_____

_____

_____

8. The Son and Spirit give what they receive, taking what they receive within the inner life of God and turning to give it to us in salvation. What does this suggest about the generous character of God?

_____

_____

_____

_____

_____

- What does this suggest about the powerful nature of our salvation?

_____

_____

_____

_____

9. List at least one thing from this chapter that stood out to you or surprised you.

_____

_____

_____

_____

_____

Use Your Imagination

You're the conductor of a symphony. The musicians are interdependent, each with a part to play in the beauty of the whole. Yet this symphony is facing some serious problems. Some musicians are intentionally playing wrong notes, introducing discord into the whole. Other musicians are playing sheet music from a different song, declaring they like that song better. Tonight is a pivotal rehearsal, with the performance coming up soon. You're preparing for your "locker room speech" before the rehearsal.

1. How will you try to convince your musicians to play together in harmony?

_____

_____

_____

_____

_____

2. What vision is compelling enough to call them out of independence and into interdependence? Describe the themes you'll address in your speech.

_____

_____

_____

_____

_____

This is an analogy for God's relation to us, as the conductor of our interdependent humanity. Humanity shares a triune, harmonic foundational structure, through the diversity-in-union of the family. This has significance for God's purposes for us as the broader international human family. Using the analogy above as a backdrop, answer the following questions.

3. If the melody is love, what human behavior might discord in the symphony represent? Give a few specific examples.

_____

_____

_____

_____

_____

4. If God is the conductor, what does "playing one's own sheet music" represent? Give some specific examples.

_____

_____

_____

_____

_____

5. If we are the musicians, why is it significant that God motivates us by beauty (a call to participate in something glorious), rather than simply control (a call to obey him just because he's in charge)?

_____

_____

_____

_____

_____

Reflect on It

1. Listen to one of your favorite songs. Consider using a worship song for this reflective exercise to center your thoughts on God, though it's not required—the bigger point is the orchestration and harmony of the music. As you listen, pay attention to the distinct parts: What instruments are playing? What notes are they contributing to the whole? What is the beat? Can you hear

the bass providing a subtle foundation beneath the surface? Are new layers added as the song progresses: a vocal harmony, a new melody line?

_____

_____

_____

_____

_____

_____

_____

2. After listening, use the space below to reflect on what specific notes God is calling you to contribute to his divine symphony. What gifts or calling has he given you? What opportunities or relationships are available to you? Are there ways you've been contributing discord? How can you orchestrate your participation in the triune symphony of humanity around God's melody of holy love?

_____

_____

_____

_____

_____

_____

_____

_____

PART VII

TRIUNE
TEMPLE

13

A RIVER RUNS THROUGH IT

Based on chapter 13 of *Beautiful Union*.

*Takeaway: The river of life is an icon of procreation
that speaks to the rise of the nations, the fruitfulness of creation,
and the work of the Spirit.*

Genesis depicts Adam's family as a mighty river—whose origins are in a sacred space where heaven and earth meet—rushing down from the cosmic mountain of God to fill the world with life. Sex is how the river moves forward. It's a vehicle for life. It's what generates the generations. Procreation produces population. The two becoming one flesh is how new flesh is formed to fill every nook and cranny of the world.

Union gives birth to life. Christ's union with his church is fruitful. God's goal is not only to dwell intimately *with* you as his bride but also to bring his abundance into the world *through* you. We are indwelt by the "river of life," the presence of God, who makes us fruitful.

There is a Trinitarian dimension to sex. If salvation is union with Christ, the kingdom is the abundant life that flows from that union. If marriage points to the work of Jesus, children point to the labor of the Spirit. The *unitive* dimension of sex points to your union with Christ; the *procreative* dimension points to your life in the Spirit. Procreation is an icon of the abundance of the kingdom.

Unpack It

1. Why were ancient civilizations built along rivers (what did the river provide)?

   _____

   _____

   _____

   - What does this background shed light on when you consider the river of life image in the Bible?

     _____

     _____

     _____

2. What relationship does sex have to the river of life and the work of the Spirit?

   _____

   _____

   _____

3. Compare the river with the tree as an icon of procreation; which icon do you lean toward?

   _____

   _____

   _____

   - What strengths do both images share?

     _____

     _____

     _____

   - What unique strengths does the river have?

     _____

     _____

     _____

- The river speaks to the fruitfulness of _____,
  the rise of the _____, and the work of the
  _____. (See page 192 in the book.)

4. Where does the first reference to infertility appear in the Bible?
   Why is this significant?

   _____

   _____

   _____

5. Name two myths the Bible confronts about infertility.

   _____

   _____

6. How can you walk well with people facing the difficult road of
   infertility?

   _____

   _____

   _____

   _____

7. When Jesus invites those who are thirsty to "come to me and
   drink," where is he standing and what day is it?[11] Why is this
   significant?

   _____

   _____

   _____

   _____

8. Jesus says, "Out of his belly will flow rivers of living water."[12]
   What is the most frequent meaning of *belly* in the New Testament? Why is this significant?

   _____

   _____

   _____

- As a living temple, what is the church's calling, and how does this meaning of *belly* point to it?

_____

_____

_____

_____

- What are some ways you and your church can live up to this calling in your relationship with Christ?

_____

_____

_____

_____

9. In the future city of God, where is the river and what does it accomplish?[13]

_____

_____

10. Sex has the power both "to *unite* lives and to *create* life."[14] Which do you see our culture emphasize more when it comes to the meaning of sex? Why do you think that is?

_____

_____

_____

_____

_____

- What role do you think procreation plays in the meaning and significance of sex?

_____

_____

_____

_____

11. List at least one thing from this chapter that stood out to you or surprised you.

_____

_____

_____

_____

_____

Use Your Imagination

Let's do an imaginative reading of Ezekiel 47:1–12. First close your eyes and take three deep breaths to prepare your heart and mind to receive the text. Then pray, *Holy Spirit, please open the eyes of my heart to receive what you have for me in your Word.*

Now, read the text and seek to place yourself in the scene, walking alongside Ezekiel during his tour of the river.

Read one verse at a time and reflect on the details, using your imagination. In verse 1, for example, how big is the temple in relation to you as you stand alongside it? How strong is the water flowing from its side? What color is the water? As you continue reading, how does the water feel on your legs when you step in? Imagine the shape and size of the fish, the types and colors of the fruit. Visualize the transformation of the Dead Sea.

1. Jot down any details that stand out to you.

_____

_____

_____

_____

2. Use the space below to reflect: Where do you need the river of the Spirit's life-giving power today? Where are the "Dead Seas" of your life, places that feel numb, empty, or hopeless? What

"trees" and "fish" do you hope for, areas of your life that might feel sparse right now where you long for divine abundance?

_____

_____

_____

_____

_____

Bring these areas before God. Listen in case the Spirit has a word, image, or other encouragement for you.

3. In what ways is God offering you his life-giving presence today?

_____

_____

_____

_____

_____

4. In what ways is God reserving this abundance now but pointing you toward the future hope of his coming kingdom?

_____

_____

_____

_____

_____

Reflect on It

Your body is about 60 percent water. It's there, even when you don't recognize it. Similarly, the Spirit sustains and upholds your existence, even when you're unaware of his presence. Reflect on ways the Spirit has sustained you that you might not have fully appreciated. It could be particular events in your life, gifts of God's good world you've received and enjoyed, or people God has used to strengthen and encourage you. Give thanks for each one, celebrating the life-giving sustenance of God.

You can survive only three days without water. Even though your body is largely composed of it, you are still dependent on receiving more of it. Similarly, even though the Spirit upholds your existence, you still need more of his presence. In what areas of your life are you thirsty for God? In what other places have you sought to satiate that thirst? Use the space below to bring your thirst before God. Ask him to fill you and quench the deeper desires of your heart with his presence.

_____

_____

_____

_____

_____

_____

_____

_____

_____

_____

_____

_____

_____

_____

_____

_____

14

ROYAL WEDDING

Based on chapter 14 of *Beautiful Union.*

Takeaway: The Song of Songs displays the iconic nature of sex, designed to represent the union you were made for with God.

———

The Song of Songs' celebration of human sexual love *magnifies* the intimacy of the union we were created for with God. As a sign of the church's union with Christ, this masterpiece *intensifies* the meaning and delight packed into the marital bliss of lovers in embrace. Properly understood, divine and human love *enhance* each other, rather than *detract* from each other.

The Song of Songs points to your identity as the bride of Christ the King. You were made to be a temple filled with his presence, a holy place washed and cleansed by his sacrifice, now with no blemish, dressed in the finest of garments, adorned with the richest of fragrance, brought to his table to dine with him and to rule and reign with him forever. Do you desire to live into this calling? This is your destiny as the bride of the King.

The gospel invites you to a royal wedding. But you're not simply invited to *attend*; you're invited to become the bride. God's not looking for you to be a spectator, an outside observer, snapping pictures with your camera while straining your neck to get a glimpse of the action. No, God's inviting you to encounter him as the great Lover of your soul, to know yourself as his beloved, to stand with him before the eyes of the watching world and be united with him in covenant forever.

Unpack It

1. What was your original understanding of the Song of Songs: a symbolic reading or a literal reading?

_____

_____

_____

_____

_____

- How does a symbolic reading of the Song of Songs elevate, rather than denigrate, the erotic dimension of human sexuality?

_____

_____

_____

_____

2. Where is the imagery for Solomon's bride taken from? Who does Solomon's bride personify?

_____

_____

- Jot down two or three details from the description of Solomon's bride that stand out to you, as well as their associations.

_____

_____

_____

3. Who does Solomon represent in the Song?

_____

_____

_____

• Jot down two or three details from Solomon's description that stand out to you, as well as their associations.

_____

_____

_____

4. How does Solomon's royal wedding point to Christ and the church?

_____

_____

_____

_____

_____

5. How does temple imagery in the Song of Songs shed light on *your* deep meaning and purpose as the bridal temple of Christ?

_____

_____

_____

_____

_____

6. What five things do circumcision and consummation have in common?

_____

_____

_____

_____

_____

• How have you thought of circumcision in the past? Has it been a confusing practice to you, or are there other associations that have stood out to you?

_____

_____

_____

_____

• How does circumcision in the Old Testament point forward to Christ's sacrifice?

_____

_____

_____

_____

7. The Song of Songs sees Scripture as a divine romance between Yahweh and his bride. Jot down two or three details from the Song that parallel the story line of Scripture.

_____

_____

_____

_____

• How is this different from seeing Scripture primarily as a legal rule book or as tips for living a better life?

_____

_____

_____

_____

• How have you perceived the story of Scripture?

_____

_____

_____

- How might your posture toward God and his story change if you saw it as a divine romance?

_____

_____

_____

8. The Day of Atonement (in Leviticus 16) is at the center of the Pentateuch. What does this suggest about the point of the Pentateuch?

_____

_____

- How does this change your understanding of the Pentateuch? Of the Bible as a whole?

_____

_____

_____

9. The gospel invites you to a wedding, but this invitation is unique: You are invited not simply to attend but to become the bride. In this season of your life, what might it look like for you to say yes and prepare for the wedding that is coming?

_____

_____

_____

_____

_____

10. List at least one thing from this chapter that stood out to you or surprised you.

_____

_____

_____

_____

Use Your Imagination

1. All right, this is going to be crazy, but bear with me. Think of your hometown or, if you prefer, the current city or location where you live. Make a list of landmarks and other things the place is known for (for example, iconic buildings, types of trees, particular animals, or types of food). Use the space below to list at least ten items.

_____

_____

_____

_____

_____

_____

2. Now your mission, should you choose to accept it, is to describe a groom and bride using the features you jotted down above. Assign at least five features to the groom and five to the bride, identifying each feature with a particular part of their person.

Groom	Bride

3. People often think of love as abstracted from geography, but relationships are rooted in a particular time and place. How might it be significant to see your relationships, and even romance, as rooted in time and place?

_____

_____

_____

_____

_____

_____

Reflect on It

You are the beloved. Single or married, male or female. In Christ, you are the beloved of God. What would it look like for you to live into this reality? To have faith not only that God exists but also that *this* is the God who exists? What lies have you believed about who God is, and who you are in Christ, that the gospel is calling you to let go of? Use the space below to reflect on what it would look like to live more fully into this reality.

_____

_____

_____

_____

_____

_____

_____

_____

_____

_____

_____

15

THE END OF THE WORLD

Based on chapter 15 of *Beautiful Union*.

Takeaway: The end of the world is a wedding,
where we shall be united with God forever.

Weddings celebrate union, and this wedding is no different. The wedding of Revelation 21–22 celebrates the union of *heaven and earth* (as God and humanity dwell together forever), the union of *east and west* (as the nations come streaming into God's holy city), the union of *weak and strong* (as the tears of the suffering and the glory of kings are received by Jesus), and the union of *good folks and bad folks* (who together belt out the song of the Lamb once slain, redeemed by the grace of God).

Our end is beautiful union. The end of the world—the goal for which it was made—is to be indwelt by the triune God. The end is love, for God is love. Our end is found in God.

In another sense, however, this end is the beginning of the world, for it shall inaugurate the end for which the world was made, the goal of our existence: to be embraced within the faithful love of God. This love shall bring forth the abundance of his kingdom, as we delight in the communion of the Trinity. The icon shall give way to the reality it pointed to all along.

We shall be united with God.

Unpack It

1. When you hear the phrase "the end of the world," what images first come to mind? Why do you think that is?

_____

_____

_____

_____

_____

2. The bride of Revelation 21 is not a person but a _____. What shape is the New Jerusalem, and what is the significance of this shape?

_____

_____

_____

_____

_____

3. How do each of the following images for the church uniquely speak to the church's calling and destiny?

     City: _____

     Temple: _____

     Bride: _____

4. The Throne, Lamb, and River describe the persons of the Trinity (the Father, Son, and Holy Spirit, respectively), as they come to indwell creation. Before reading this book, how did you view the Trinity?

_____

_____

_____

_____

- What, if anything, has changed in how you view the Trinity?

  _____

  _____

  _____

- What stands out to you about the hope that the Throne, Lamb, and River offer the world?

  _____

  _____

  _____

5. You prepare for the end of the world by becoming a lover of God. How does this contrast with other "doomsday preparation" scenarios?

  _____

  _____

  _____

  _____

  _____

6. List at least one thing from this chapter that stood out to you or surprised you.

  _____

  _____

  _____

  _____

  _____

Use Your Imagination

There is no shortage of movies and novels exploring the end of the world. The entire post-apocalyptic genre envisions something disastrous—nuclear holocaust, an alien invasion, a meteor striking the earth—that brings everything to a crashing end.

1. What movie or novel first comes to mind when you think of the end of the world? In one paragraph, write down the plot. Try to recall the major scenes, characters, and details, as best as you can.

_____

_____

_____

_____

_____

_____

2. Why do you think people are fascinated by such end-of-the-world scenarios? What is it about them that captures the imagination and speaks to the human condition? Why do you think we assume the end will be a disaster? What does this say about the hope of the world on our own resources, apart from God?

_____

_____

_____

_____

_____

3. Now, contrast these scenarios with the biblical depiction of the end of the world as a wedding. How does this hope contrast with the scenarios mentioned above? What does this suggest about where—and where alone—true hope can be found? What does the symbol of a wedding suggest about the nature of this hope?

_____

_____

_____

_____

_____

Reflect on It

You were made for God. That is your highest calling, your deepest purpose, where your greatest longings will be fulfilled. You might feel like hope is lost. Like the world is too far gone. But the gospel says you can lift your eyes in hope. A wedding is coming, and it's a wedding that will heal the world.

This is how you prepare for the end of the world: by becoming a lover of God. What would it look like to live into this reality? To prepare for this destiny? To make Christ your highest priority, the love above all loves, the greatest excellency to which nothing else can compare? Use the space below to reflect on how you can prepare for that future today.

_____

_____

_____

_____

_____

_____

_____

_____

_____

_____

_____

_____

_____

_____

FINAL THOUGHTS

We need a new sexual revolution. One driven not by the freedom to do what we want but by the freedom to reflect who God is. Not by the dry legalism of rule keeping but by the deeper human vocation of image bearing. Not by the objectifying use of the other in self-love but by the sincere giving of the self in a communion of love.

This revolution is for all of us. Single or married, male or female, divorced or widowed, rich or poor, from a loving family or a broken home. Whatever your history, your heartbreaks, your suspicions, your circumstances, your inclinations, your longings, this vision is for you because Jesus is for you. You can have the reality—with or without the sign—for the message contained in sex is available in Christ to all who would receive him.

As you come to the close of this book, pause for a moment and consider everything you've learned. What have been your biggest takeaways? Use the space below to reflect on a key theological insight, a key practical takeaway, and anything else that made a significant impact on you.

NOTES

1. This phrase is adapted from Sam Allberry, *7 Myths About Singleness* (Wheaton, Ill.: Crossway, 2019), 120.

2. Genesis 1:27.

3. Matthew 6:10.

4. John 17:24.

5. Michael Reeves unpacks this powerful observation in his excellent book *Delighting in the Trinity: An Introduction to the Christian Faith* (Downers Grove, Ill.: IVP Academic, 2012), 19–38.

6. Matthew 19:6, NIV.

7. Matthew 11:30.

8. Psalm 68:5–6, NIV.

9. *Black Mirror*, season 3, episode 1, "Nosedive," directed by Joe Wright, written by Rashida Jones and Michael Schur, aired October 21, 2016.

10. Genesis 1:27.

11. John 7:37.

12. John 7:38. I've rendered *koilias* as "belly," matching the King James Version and the most common definition of the term; *A Greek-English Lexicon of the New Testament* (New York: Harper, 1894), "koilia," 2836.

13. Revelation 21–22.

14. Todd Wilson, *Mere Sexuality: Rediscovering the Christian Vision of Sexuality* (Grand Rapids, Mich.: Zondervan, 2017), 97.

Discover the Beautiful Invitation of Our Sexuality as God Intended It to Be

A provocative yet practical look at what God has to say about sex and what sex reveals about God.

Dig into the Bible's beautiful narrative about what our sexuality is intended to point us toward in this dynamic companion guide to the book.